5

Anytime Resolutions

Your New Year Doesn't Have

To Begin In January

CHANIN RICHEL

Chanin Richel, LLC

www.chaninrichel.com

5 Anytime Resolutions

Your New Year Doesn't Have To Begin In January

Printed in the United States of America

Chanin Richel, LLC
9300 Meadowfield Court
Richmond, VA 23060

www.chaninrichel.com

Cover design by Pro Ebook Cover Designs
Copyedited by Lauren Pilgrim and Penny Hembrick
Author photograph by Patterson | Evans

Published by Chanin Richel, LLC

Table of Contents

DEDICATION

This book is dedicated to Vivian Pilgrim. To know her was to love her. I will forever miss her dedication, understanding, patience and humor.

This book is also dedicated to the rest of my family. There is no better feeling than being able to just be yourself. Nothing can replace the hilarious birthday parties, cookouts, and just becauses' that we share.

My favorite quote about family perfectly describes us

–

"Families are like fudge, mostly sweet with a few nuts"

I love you ALL!

Introduction

I am so happy that you decided to take the first step towards creating the life that you desire! This interactive book is a simple combination of common sense and life skills that we all sometimes lose sight of due to life's circumstances.

You have a right to be happy and to live your best life! Sometimes though, life's circumstances lead us to a place where we're anything but that. Often we find ourselves at the end of the day, tired and feeling like we've just been treading on a wheel for hours without actually going anywhere. Stresses like debt, relationships and job plans play on our mind. We feel depressed and end up buying a bunch of things we don't need, distancing ourselves emotionally, lashing out at people close to us, or zoning out in front of the television to try and forget about it all.

We spend too much time scrolling through 'Instagrammed' photos or status updates on Facebook. Many of us are only living a fulfilled and exciting life in "Cyber Land." Most of the time we give the robotic answer of 'Great!' when asked how we are. We don't realize that there are some basic life principals that, when combined with a slight attitude adjustment, can bring us to that true place of satisfaction and accomplishment! If this is you, you are not alone.

If you really want to change your life, you're going to have to take responsibility for it yourself. You have to ask yourself the hard questions and take steps – even small ones – in the right direction. You are the one essential ingredient in your own life change. If you don't show up prepared to do the hard work, no amount of book reading or dreaming is going to help you. Only you can do that.

When I started writing this book I was over $50,000 in debt and working a job where I had reached my ceiling. It wasn't until I started practicing techniques that you will find in this book that I realized I could change things if I wanted to. Now I'm living out my passion every day and feeling truly fulfilled.

As you are reading this book and you hear me talk about *"your best life"* or *"your best self,"* I mean the one that YOU want to live - the relationship YOU dream of, a job or business YOU wake up to every morning with anticipation, a supportive group of friends or the ability to look in the mirror and smile at yourself – whichever combination of wonderful life circumstances you want to pursue, it can be yours.

You will discover how to make transforming changes to your everyday activities that will empower you to fully embrace life. You will discover how to take control of your mind, your relationships, your finances and your life direction. I will show you those techniques that worked for me and have worked for thousands of others.

So what is the first step? Turn the page... (See, I told you the steps were simple!)

"Change Is Not Change, Until You Change"

Chapter 1

Renewing The Mind

The process of renewing the mind is serious business. Out of everything that you will read in this book, renewing your mind is the most important. It's not easy to get rid of "stinking thinking" and gain a new way of looking at yourself and the world. It requires a lot of hard work, but I know that if you are really serious about changing your life, you can do it! Through this book I'm going to *help* you do it, step by step.

Here we go...

There once was a father who had twin girls. Even though they were identical physically, each one had a very different personality and approach to life. One year he decided to conduct an experiment at Christmas. He put each girl in a different room with a bunch of presents. The first one opened her presents: designer clothes, iPod and video games. With a small sigh she started complaining about each one and predicting it would soon break or wasn't as good as her friends'. In the other room, he found his other daughter surrounded by the pile of manure he had carefully wrapped in bright Christmas paper, grinning from ear to ear. "Daddy!" she said, shivering with excitement. "With all this manure... did you get me a horse for Christmas?"

What made the difference between the two girls, apart from the obvious fact that one girl was happy and the other was miserable?

The difference is a hugely important aspect of our humanity known as a *mindset*. Understanding it and controlling it will literally change your life.

What Is A Mindset?

A mindset is the way that you look at the world and how you react to the things that happen to you. One of the twin girls always saw the negative side of a situation and so she was constantly miserable. The other twin girl always saw the positive side of a situation and was constantly a lot happier.

Your mindset determines how much you get out of life, decides the way you interpret events in your life, and dictates how you will respond to them. It also changes how you interpret other people's actions towards you.

Often, simply by changing our mindset, we can change our life. This is because when we see things differently (*possible* instead of *impossible*, *accepting* instead of *rejecting*, *open* instead of *closed*) we react in a different way and that changes the way the world responds to us.

EXERCISE: Walk down the street frowning and look angrily at people. What sort of reactions do you get in return? Does it seem like there are a lot of rude and angry people in the world? Now turn around and walk the other way smiling at people. What a difference! Maybe some of them thought you were weird but I'll bet that many of them returned the smile because of your beautiful, smiling face. Your mindset will cause you to experience a series of negative or positive reactions that genuinely affect the way you view the world around you.

Where Does A Mindset Come From?

The great news is that a mindset is largely determined by external forces. For most of us, our mindset is based on family traditions, religious traditions or our environment. Traditions can be helpful in giving us rituals to ground ourselves in or events to look forward to, but can really hold us back in freeing us into our best possible life. This is because our mindset is such an embedded part of us that we're often not even aware of it and just let it carry us along wherever it may take us.

I was raised in Richmond, VA, along with my brother, by two strong Christian women both of whom attended Virginia Union University. My grandmother was a woman who refused to tell us how to spell any word or give us information that we could look up on our own. If we wanted to know *anything* we needed to become acquainted with Mr. Dictionary and Mrs. Encyclopedia. Then there was my mom. She didn't let grass grow under our feet and took us anywhere that her little Jetta could go. We were well-rounded kids who had no idea that we were poor. We grew up in an Income Based Housing project called Newbridge Village and it was riddled with drugs, fighting and killing. While it was clear that we were good kids, I have to consider that our environment did have an effect on us. Neither one of us attended a 4-year college nor did we place a value on homeownership while we were growing up.

ANSWER THIS: How did you grow up? What kind of environment was it? How has it affected your decisions, as you grew older?

Now, I am in the process of purchasing my first home and I am so proud to give to organizations that encourage fresh starts like Dress for Success. On top of that, I get to live a life where I help others discover their best selves through motivational talks as well as direct my own destiny through personal business endeavors.

Along the way, I've had to renew my mindset a number of times. That's right – take it to the drycleaners to get it washed up and straightened out. These times of renewing my mind were crucial to my own ability to realize my full potential and enjoy the journey along the way. You can do it too.

How Do I Change My Mindset?

I'm so glad you asked! As with everything, it is a journey and a journey is made up of a few steps, one after the after. Start with these...

Step 1: Connect or Reconnect with God

Your first step is to reconnect or get connected with God, the One who created you and knows you best.

I believe it is important to start here because you need a foundation. You need something solid to build your life on and that means making time to connect with your Creator your number one priority.

EXERCISE: List two things you can do to begin a relationship or get back in touch with God. Some people go to church, some people worship Him through music, some spend time in meditation or maybe you can start by reading the Bible. www.biblegateway.com is a great tool that offers daily scriptures and access to the Bible online.

I want you to schedule the 2 things that you listed into your week right now.

During this process you may be surprised to find that you lose a few friends and even family members. When I reconnected with God (after a period of straying away) in an attempt to find my own path, I did not spend a lot of time with a lot of people. I spent most of it by myself and with God. The reason for this is that you need to clear your mind and your heart to be able to focus your energy on what is important. Don't get me wrong, the husband/wife is important, the kids are important, the dog, your friends... okay I think you get the point. They are all very important parts of our life, however, to continue to give your best to your loved ones you need to make time alone with God a priority for a while.

Step 2: Find out what the Bible says about you

The New Testament is full of incredible truths about our identity as part of God's family.

EXERCISE: Open your bible and write out passages that God has uses to speak to you about your identity and purpose in life.

Need somewhere to get started? How about these:

You are a child of God

But to all who have received Him–those who believe in His name–He has given the right to become God's children (John 1:12).

You are more than a conqueror

We are more than conquerors through Him that loved us (Romans 8:37).

You can do all things

I can do all things through Christ Jesus, which strengthens me (Philippians 4:13).

God loves you

For God so loved the world that He gave His only begotten Son (John 3:16).

Step 3: Watch what goes in your brain and what comes out your mouth

Your brain is just like a computer; it receives instructions and acts on them. Words are like the brain's keyboard. Songs you listen to, people you hang around and especially the words you say are typed like commands into the computer--your brain. Your brain then takes these commands and files and stores them away as information affecting your identity and mindset. This is a powerfully underestimated mechanism of the brain. The brain doesn't recognize when we are being sarcastic or if words we hear are not about us but rather some person in a song. It hears words and it acts on them.

So when you say, 'I'm just over everything at the moment or nothing goes right for me.' Your brain says, 'Oh, we are over everything at the moment' and sends depressed hormones through your system. Then it also notes that 'Nothing goes right for us' and files a note not to bother trying because it won't work out anyway.

It is crucial that you keep the things you listen to and the things you say in line with the future you want to create for yourself. Keep your brain working with you, not against you and renew your mind with positive words about yourself and the people around you. There are wonderful teachings about the power of your mind by the authors of The Secret.

Step 4: Have High Self-Esteem

There was an experiment done that revealed the natural lack of self-esteem in most of the population. Two advertisements were placed in a newspaper (yes – it was a very old experiment!) with no more detail than "WORKER WANTED" and the salary. One advertisement listed the salary at

$40,000/year. The other advertisement listed the salary at $400,000/year. How many applicants do you think applied for each one?

You would assume that most people asked for information about the job with the higher salary right? After all, there was no criteria specified that would disqualify anyone, regardless of their work history. Interestingly enough, that wasn't the case. Over 2500 inquiries were received for the lower salary advertisement. Only 6 inquiries were received for the higher salary advertisement.

Why? People discounted themselves based on their past experiences and what other people had told them they were worth. They were not used to thinking of themselves as worthy of a $400,000/year job and so didn't even bother to apply. They had pre-rejected themselves.

"You miss 100% of all the shots you don't take."

Don't pre-reject yourself. You are the only one responsible for believing in yourself. How do you know what you are capable of until you have tried? The way you think of yourself is a choice, one that you daily cement into your mindset with the phrases you tell yourself. 'I probably won't even get an interview.' 'They're not going to like me.'

EXERCISE: If you haven't already, start taking special note of your mental reaction to challenging situations. What are you telling yourself about yourself? Write down some of the things you often think about yourself.

Now ask yourself, "Is it kind, Is it necessary, Is it true?"

– Suze Orman

Renewing your mind is not a one-day or one-time process. It is a continual effort to take control of your thinking patterns and perception of events around you. Like jewelry, it gets tarnished from continual interaction with a messy and negative world. Remember to take time regularly to renew your mind in order to keep moving in the direction of the life that you desire.

Chapter 2

Filtering People

Filtering people is not an easy process and most people do not enjoy it. However, successful people know that it is a necessary process for moving into the life that they want to live.

In order for you to do this, it requires you to have a high sense of self-worth. Filtering allows you to remove people from your life that have a "one-way street" view of your relationship. Meaning that they only want to be around you for the reasons that benefit themselves.

The people we hang out with are hugely important to the direction our life takes.

Have you ever heard that saying, 'You are what you eat?' Well, it's also true that you are who you hang out with, "Birds of a feather, flock together." Our brains naturally pick up the attitudes and approaches to life of the people we hang out with the most. They are either increasing your energy and positivity or they are decreasing your spirit and belief in yourself.

Sometimes when we hear the term "filtering people" we hear: callously ridding ourselves of anyone who does not immediately benefit us or burning bridges. I didn't say burning bridges in the manner we sometimes do when we've just "had enough". I said filtering. This sort of cutting off of a relationship is usually messy, takes a lot of emotional energy and leaves both parties feeling awkward if they ever accidentally run into each other.

3 Degrees Of Connection

Filtering is a much more gentle process of separation by degrees. Those degrees are Inner Circle, Friends, and Acquaintances. The definition of filtering is – "Passing through a device to remove unwanted material." This is what successful people do with the relationships in their lives; they have a device that keeps out unwanted material...A.K.A people from their inner world.

Inner Circle: We are all made up of layers of intimacy; our closest feelings, dreams, hopes and devastations are shared with people we trust and feel safe with. We invest a lot into them and they invest a lot into us. It may be a family member, a best friend or a neighbor that you have lived next to for years.

Friends Circle: Outside of the Inner Circle is the Friends Circle. Those we rely on for after-work drinks, the occasional word of advice and to show up to our baby's first birthday party. Often, these are the friends who you may lose touch with when they move away or change jobs. Some will stick around and eventually make their way to the inner circle.

Acquaintances Circle: Outside of the Friends Circle is the Acquaintances Circle. Those we get along with and are maybe Facebook friends with because your kids play on the same team or you went to a movie with mutual friends once. They might be happy to help you out with a recommendation for a good holiday spot or even for a favor picking up the kids from school once, but you'd never expect them to devote time and energy to your well-being. They are so far down your list of phone numbers, that you have to think to even remember their name.

The wonderful thing about these circles is that the communication, support and love go both ways. While giving friendship to someone else, there's also the opportunity for him or her to give friendship in return.

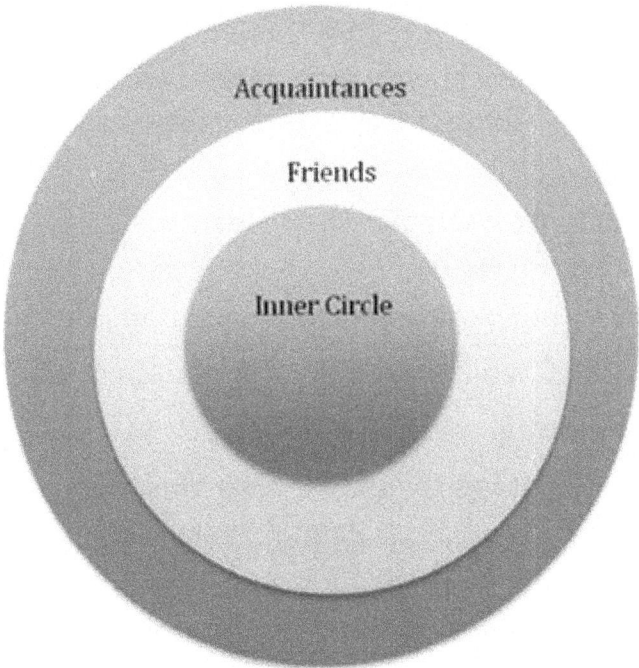

EXERCISE: Draw three circles, one inside the other, on a piece of paper. List the names of people in your world who fall into each category. Are there any you're not sure about? Write their names on the side of your paper and ask yourself what role they play in your life if they are not in one of the 3 Circles.

Now, let's look at how I can help you define who should stay in your Inner Circle.

An Inner Circle Deficiency

What happens when these relationships get out of balance? I'm not talking about mentoring or children. In these relationships it is clear that one person is the primary giver and the other the taker. I'm talking about what happens when one relationship is pulling a lot of energy from your intimate inner circle *without replenishing it.*

We all know the person who never bothers to call you until he or she needs something. Someone always "promising to catch up" but is never actually available. I'm sure you've had this happen to you. We all have the friend who is constantly in a dramatic crisis, even when you're having your own genuine crisis. These interactions draw on our energies, requiring time and effort that reduces our own emotional capacity. Usually the same person who took it out replenishes this, but sometimes someone in your life stops giving back. What happens then?

BEFORE YOU KEEP READING: Do you have anyone in your world like this right now? Write their name down on your piece of paper.

You probably guessed what happens: An inner circle deficiency. That relationship is draining you. How long can it go on until you don't have enough energy to replenish yourself? How long until you can't keep yourself with a positive point of view and you start giving in to challenges instead of fighting them?

Happy and fulfilled people take control of their degrees of connection instead of allowing others to ping in and out of their intimate circle. They are the determinants for how much each person will draw of their energy. This way, they always know that they are full of their own vitality to continue giving and growing personally.

How Do I Filter My Relationships?

I typically do this once a year: I take off the last 2 weeks of each year and spend quality time at home to think about what happened during the current year and make plans for the upcoming year.

The first week I spend time going over what I did during the current year. Did I meet my goals? Did I waste time on things that were not productive? Who did I spend the majority of my time with?

The second week I spend time going over the new goals that I would like to set for the upcoming year. What would I like to accomplish? Is there anything that I need to change from the previous year? **Last but not least, I also include the filtering process.**

I look back to see who picks up the phone to call me as much as I call them. Who can I talk to when I have had a bad day instead of just listening to someone else's problems? I decide who, of all my friends, replenishes my energy just as much as I replenish theirs. Then I make a resolution to keep those people in my inner circle and move the others to a less intimate circle.

It doesn't mean I cut them off completely. I'm still friendly if they ever call. I will even respond to the occasional call for assistance if they need it, but I'm NOT making any effort to get closer to them. I have had to move a couple of people from my inner circle – declining invitations to events and not engaging in deeper conversations when they start due to the "one-way street" view that they have of our relationship.

This can be difficult. It takes realizing that it is your decision whether this person gets to be a part of your life or not. It takes the ability to recognize when someone is draining you rather than replenishing you.

There is a great book, by John Gordon titled The Energy Bus, that has a section on "No Energy Vampires" that I really like that gives great tips on avoiding people that drain you in your personal life as well as on your job.

EXERCISE: Return to the person you listed as someone in your inner circle that takes more than he or she gives. What would happen if you stopped making an effort to talk and spend time with them? Perhaps that person needs to be in the 'Friends' circle or the 'Acquaintances' circle.

The time that used to be spent calling or emailing can now be used for much more productive purposes! What's more, you have time and mental energy for new people who *do* replenish your inner circle and are as interested in building a friendship with you as you are with them.

Nurture those relationships and keep others in the outer circles.

Chapter 3

Do You Need To Downsize?

L et me warn you now, you are NOT going to like this chapter. No one wants to hear that they need to get rid of their prized possessions or that they need to save more money.

When I started on this journey of being able to live out my life with purpose I had to go through this process myself. I was $56,000 in debt due to a nasty divorce mixed with poor decision making and it was starting to keep me up at night. It was time to do something about it.

When trying to live out your purpose, it is extremely important to get rid of any extra baggage that may stand in the way of you achieving your purpose. As discussed in the previous chapter, filtering needs to happen not only with people, but it also needs to happen with things. When you are living above your means, you are under a constant pressure to maintain "The Things."

Living debt free, with the exception of your home, allows you the freedom to explore life without the pressure of "I owe, I owe, it's off to work I go." The financial strain of credit cards, big car notes, and fancy clothes are the biggest enemy of living a debt-free life -- with purpose.

What Really Makes You Happy?

We are constantly being sold an idea that what really makes us happy is *more stuff*. Magazines and television shows portray people in expensive stuff, looking happy and contented in life. According to marketing psychology, people connect happiness with things and believe – **believe, mind you** – that the stuff is the cause of the happiness. This is the very basis that advertising is built on.

However, studies have shown that beyond a certain point, more money doesn't make a person happy. This is because stuff doesn't make us happy. Humans typically feel a spike of happiness immediately after the purchase but the joy quickly dissipates, leaving a feeling of emptiness.

What does make us happy? Purpose in our life, physical health and solid relationships are far more conducive to a state of well-being than a 70" television and nice clothes. Put down the magazines and focus on yourself for a moment.

EXERCISE: On the top of a piece of paper describe a moment when you were truly happy. On the left side of the paper, write down the physical things involved in that situation. On the right side, write the immaterial things in that situation. For instance, if your happy moment is laughing with a friend during after-work drinks, on the left side you might write, 'Money for drinks, clothes to wear, taxi money to get home.' On the right side you would write, 'Friend time, relaxed mind, health'.

MY HAPPY MOMENT: New Year's Eve with friends at Stacey's	
MATERIAL STUFF	**IMMATERIAL STUFF**
New dress	Friends
Bottle of wine	Healthy body
Taxi to get home	Relaxed mind

Now, on the left side, ask which of these things you could have replaced with other things and still had a good time. Could you have had wine at home instead of in a bar? YES. Did the fact that you were wearing Gucci shoes make you laugh more? NO.

We can have happy times with just a small amount of stuff. It is true that we DO need some money to enjoy life but not as much as the magazines and television tell us. Your Challenge -- Be More With Less

Here are some steps I took to get myself out of debt:

Step 1 - Find A Mentor

Find someone to partner with who has different spending habits than you. You need to find someone who has a proven track record of success in this area. Just so that we are clear, driving the newest model Mercedes or living in the biggest house on the street does not mean that person is successful. They may be "house poor" and have a ton of debt trying to "keep up with the Jones"!

I am talking about someone who is willing to show you exactly how and what he or she did to get to the point in their life where they have what they want and need. Do they use a family budget? If so, how did they come up with it? How much do they add to a savings account or IRA account monthly? Who do they bank with and why?

Ask yourself: Who do you have in your life that is excellent with managing money? Make a list of at least three people. Send an e-mail or text message to that person right now asking them to catch up and get some advice. Afraid? Don't be! People love giving advice. It's a compliment. Suggest meeting at a Starbucks and pay for their coffee to say thank you.

I had the pleasure of spending months being mentored by my aunt. We spent many hours talking about living within your means, correcting poor spending habits, how to save, how to budget and how to build up retirement accounts. During this time I listened very carefully and followed all of the advice given to me. The steps were easy to follow and very practical. If you do not have anyone in your life that you feel is qualified to give you this advice, I would suggest watching Suze Orman. She is very knowledgeable about finances and comes on every Saturday night. You can even write in to her show to ask questions and get advice.

Step 2 – Set Goals

Finances are as simple as what goes out must come in. A budget is the only way to ensure you are living within your means. The first step in any financial management is to clarify exactly what income you have coming in and what expenses must go out. Many people try to complicate this step but the key is to keep it simple. When it's as simple as 'what goes out, must come in', it is not difficult.

EXCERCISE: A budget is as simple as income on one side and expenses on the other. Using either an excel spreadsheet or a budget tool like Suze Orman has here or even just a plain piece of paper, write down your income on the left side and your regular monthly expenses on the other side. Use your credit card and bank statements. It's the little things we forget about that add up, like insurance or bank fees. Your bank may offer online banking with budgeting tools. I always recommend banking with a Credit Union because they offer very personal service. They also offer budgeting and educational tools online for free.

Now that you know where your current spending is, it's time to decide where you want it to be. This is the point at which you will want to pull in your mentor. Show them your current financial state–don't be shy! Share with them your dream of financial freedom and then work backwards from your ultimate goal, developing milestones that are progressively achievable.

Don't forget the rewards! While paying off debt and having savings in the bank have its own reward, you will also need rewards that satisfy your other desires for enjoyment of life, like holidays or new shoes. Decide what is important for you. Find something that will motivate you to stick to your budget and place a reminder of it somewhere prominent – a picture on your bedroom wall for instance.

Step 3 – Pay Off Debt

If you currently have debt, you need to accept the reality that you have been living beyond your means. PERIOD! To pay it off and to gain the peace of mind and financial freedom that comes from never paying interest, you will need to change your spending habits. There may be items you can do without, for instance, a fancy car. Maybe you have a wardrobe full of clothes, shoes or electronics you no longer use that you can sell. If you have debt in multiple areas, like a car loan and multiple credit cards, you may be able to consolidate them into one easy payment with a lower interest rate through a financial assistance service. If you need help getting started you can contact someone at The Association of Independent Consumer Credit Counseling Agencies.

You will never get out of debt while you have the false security of a credit card in your purse or wallet. Here's a newsflash - you can actually survive without the credit card! That way you're not flushing your money down the interest toilet.

Paying down debt will make you feel great! Just make sure you're not tempted to build it back up again. Buying those new shoes on your credit card is not a good reward for paying off your credit card! Refer to Step 2 and make sure you have rewards already planned out in advance.

Step 4 – Build Up Your Savings

Even if you have debt you should not ignore starting a savings fund. While it may make logical sense to pay down debt as quickly as possible, building up a savings account will keep your motivation strong. Seeing dollars build up that are yours and actually earning you money by just sitting there is a great reminder of your future financial freedom. Your goal for your savings account should ultimately be to have enough cash to support you for at least eight months to a year in an emergency.

It is best to set up automatic transfers immediately after income lands in your bank account. This way, the money is not there for you to accidentally spend. Automating your budget as much as possible will remove stress.

Step 6 – Find New Income Streams

Lastly, try your hand at discovering new income streams for your life. Cutting back on going out on the weekends or shopping every Saturday afternoon, will give you time to explore your creativity and discover how you can provide value to the world. The rise of the Internet has opened up potential new income streams even for hobbyists. Sites like Etsy.com and eBay.com allows anyone with a good idea for a product or service to find potential buyers. In the next chapter we're going to talk about finding and discovering your purpose. Many businesses were created from a unique, creative product!

What Can You Do With A Debt-Free Life?

You Can Spend When The Time Is Right

When you have a large amount of savings and no debt, you can choose to spend money at times that actually save you money. For instance, you can buy winter clothes at the end of the winter season when they are all on sale. Or, if you want to purchase a car, Cash Is King! You have the upper hand on negotiations when you have cash as opposed to needing financing. On a larger scale, you can take the opportunity of a downturn in the real estate market to buy an investment. Some people think that credit cards give us this opportunity. But credit cards come with a cost.

EXERCISE: Get out your credit card statements and add up how much money you have spent on interest this year write that amount down on a piece of paper. This is how much money you could have put into a savings account. Pin this up somewhere so that you can see it to remind you of the cost of credit cards.

You Can Choose For Love Not Money

So many people today work in jobs they hate simply because it pays the bills. 40 hours of a workweek is spent in an environment that sucks the joy right out of their life, just to be able to come home exhausted and watch a movie on a bigger-than-usual screen. Being debt free allows you to take a job that maybe pays a little less but which you truly enjoy. Now, 40 hours of your week are spent enjoying life and you have energy left over for a walk in the park instead of zoning out in front of the 70" tv.

You Can Reduce Stress

If you've ever had your credit card declined at a counter, you'll know what I mean when I say that living beyond your means creates stress. Your brain responds to stress by producing adrenaline that increases your heart rate and makes it difficult to relax. Stress reduces libido, makes it difficult to focus and clouds your thinking. Getting rid of stress frees your mind to take you in the direction of your purposeful life.

You Can Take A Risk To Get What You Really Want

Would you like to write a book? Work as a volunteer overseas? Help your sister with her education? Start a business? Having a lot of money in savings gives you the freedom to take a risk and give your dream wings. You never know what could happen...

You Can Give To Those Around You

When you are out of debt you can become someone who is "Blessed to be a Blessing." Seeing other people expand their lives with the finances you have provided is one of life's best experiences and makes you a good steward of what you have already been given. Whether your heart is to give to your local church or some other cause, being debt-free allows you to be a generous, full-hearted giver.

Now do you have a better understanding of the importance of downsizing and saving money? Because how can you take a leap of faith to live the life that you desire and pursue your passion when you are tied down by debt?

Chapter 4

Determining Your Purpose

Now that we have discussed renewing your mind, filtering people that drain your energy without replenishing it, downsizing things that you don't need and streamlining your finances, it's time to start focusing on your **purpose**. Believe it or not, this is actually where you get to have some fun! You are going to explore what gets your blood pumping!

Can you remember a situation when it seemed as though time had stopped? Maybe you were engrossed in a project or talking with a friend about a particular subject. Maybe you looked away from the computer screen or happened to glance at the clock in a lull in the conversation and suddenly realized, 'Oh my goodness! It's 3 AM!'

I love that feeling of waking up to the excitement and anticipation of the activities on my agenda for the day... even when I haven't had enough sleep. When we're working on something that is our passion, we always seem to have energy. Compare that to the feeling you get when a task before you is not your passion; that slow dread seeping into your chest when you wake up every morning, the sigh as you sit down to the task and the incredibly slow movement of time as you glance at the clock every five minutes expecting an hour to have gone past.

So, now it is time for you to begin your journey toward discovering your purpose. This is one of the greatest journeys a person can ever take. Ever since I can remember, I have been giving advice and helping others, and I love it! For some strange reason when I am helping others or giving advice I completely forget about myself and any issues that I may have going on in my personal life. If you did a survey among people who regularly volunteer, I'm sure that they will say the same thing. I found my purpose – Life Coaching to help others become their best self! I had been "Life Coaching" my whole life and never knew that there were people who did this for a living.

Discovering your life purpose can sometimes take a lifetime. Regardless of how long this journey takes, it's great to remember that the joy of life, is as much in the journey, as it is in reaching the goal. Discovering your purpose will involve discovering many different passions along the way. Don't get so caught up in trying to reach the goal of 'Your Purpose,' that you miss out on the joy that comes from the journey of finding out what it is.

Here are some steps to get you started on discovering your passion:

Step 1 – Find And Understand Your Passion

Find a place where you feel comfortable and your mind is free. Take a notebook or a laptop and begin making a list of what you love to do!

Think back to moments that seemed to move very quickly for you or that you had a lot of anticipation for. Don't limit yourself just to those moments that are considered traditional work. Perhaps you have nieces or nephews that you love spending time with. *Maybe your passion is working with children.* Do you go for nature walks? *Maybe your passion is working in the environment.* How about sports played on the weekend? *Maybe your passion is sports related.* If you were to suddenly find yourself a billionaire with no need to earn money, how would you spend your time? Many people think they would retire, relax and drink martinis on the beach. Actually, most people would get bored with a lifestyle like that. As humans we love a challenge. What challenges excite you? Write them down. The challenges you write down may be very general or very specific. You might write something general like volunteering or you might write something quite specific like committing to the Peace Corps overseas for two years. Write everything! Push yourself to write down at least 15 things.

It's important to understand why you enjoy an activity. For example, let's look at website designers: some people love designing websites because they enjoy the process of designing and creating. Others love working on websites because they truly believe in the cause behind the website and are excited about how it can change the world. Still others work on websites because they like the freedom and flexibility they get from being a freelancer. And yet, others enjoy it because they can hang around with other tech savvy people.

Understanding the why behind your enjoyment will help lead you to your passion.

Step 2 – Get Clear On Your Priorities

Wouldn't it be great if we could do everything in life we are passionate about? I would love to tell you to take that list of 15 things and just go out and make it happen! Unfortunately, life doesn't work like that. That is why it's vital to get clear on what you are *most* passionate about!

EXERCISE: Look at your list of 15 things that challenge you. Rank the top 3. This will keep you from being a 'Jack of all trades and a master of none.'

Step 3 – Test The Waters

In a study conducted to discover how people successfully changed careers, it was clarified that the people who discovered their passion after a period of searching for it, didn't just sit at home thinking about it. They made it their goal to try as many potential courses of action as possible. This included short study courses, internships, attending conferences, asking to meet with someone who was already performing a role they were considering and taking positions on new projects. **Your passion is not going to appear out of thin air!** Most likely it will develop slowly as you change your life towards those things that fulfill you, rather than just those things that help you get by.

EXERCISE: Make a list of 5 things you can do to get started. Something is better than nothing!

Not everyone has the guts to pursue a fulfilling purpose. Just by reading this book, you've taken the first step and that tells me that you are the sort of person who can actively pursue the things you want in life. Finding and living your purpose will bring you greater fulfillment than any other goal, including money and job titles. It's time to get to it!

Chapter 5

Do It Afraid

Now that you've identified your top 3 passions and made a plan to test the waters...it's time to DO IT AFRAID!

It's not always easy leaving your comfort zone. Many of us have taken the same route --to the same job – with the same people – for 10 years or more. If you still work full-time and have vacation time available, you should begin using it for your transition to pursuing your passion. Take that class, volunteer at a local non-profit agency or use that time to organize and implement activities for the next 90 days.

I started one day at a time. To be honest, the first couple of times that I took a day off from work I had to continue to remind myself that "the office is not going to fall apart just because I am not there." When I had an upcoming day off, I started looking online to see if there were any classes that I wanted to take, were there any volunteer opportunities that I was interested in or was there something on my "to do" list that I could accomplish that was a part of my goals. One of my major goals was to write this book. I had been putting it off for years. I was afraid that no one would want to read what I had to say because I was not qualified with any college degrees. But strangely enough even though I don't have a college degree or a bunch of accolades, people always come to me for advice and ask my opinion about everyday life situations. Before I knew it I was being asked to speak on a panel in front of hundreds of women. If you have ever met me, you would not know that I am very shy and terrified of speaking in front of people. I could choose to back out of the opportunities due to being out of my comfort zone or I could take my own advice and "Do It Afraid."

Doing it afraid does not have to be scary, but you may get nervous and experience butterflies in your stomach. That just means you're headed in the right direction. I heard a quote once that could not be more of a true statement – "If your dream doesn't scare you, it is not big enough." –Kristine Stevens

Whatever it is that you want to do, go for it. If you have something that you want to accomplish, just put one foot in front of the other. You may even make mistakes but consider it all a part of the learning process. If people say that you can't do it, use that as fuel to drive you even harder to accomplish your dreams. Most of the time they are only saying that because they don't have enough vision to see themselves doing more than what they are currently doing (or have been doing for the past 20 years)!

Sometimes when we receive new information or ideas we just sit on them. This especially seems to happen when it comes to reading books. Some of us are serial book readers. We just read one book after another and never really DO anything. Why is this? This is because it is easy to just *read* a self-help book. However, it takes courage and discipline to actually *do the work* that is required to gain whatever change it is that you are seeking for your life.

I know how hard it is. I had to do it step-by-step:

~ Reconnecting With God

~ Filtering People

~ Downsizing From Unnecessary "Things"

~ Determining My Purpose

~ And finally Doing It Afraid

Pursuing your passion should be fun and exciting. I now feel fulfilled in being able to help people discover their own purpose and gain freedom from debt and the limiting beliefs that they hold about themselves. I hope that by sharing the tips that I took to restore my life, you too will find that you are able to focus on finding the life that you desire. Make a commitment to wake up everyday determined to live on purpose.

What are you waiting for? The only thing left to do is to "Do It Afraid."

About The Author

Chanin Richel is an Author, CEO & Creative Director of Chanin Richel LLC, a fashion design company based in Richmond, VA.

After graduating High School, she studied modeling and acting at John Casablanca's, an internationally known modeling and entertainment agency. In addition, Chanin worked in the top hair salon in Richmond, Virginia that afforded her the opportunity to interact with other trend setting professionals through hair and beauty shows and day-to-day customer contact and service. Those interactions fostered and nurtured a desire to begin designing and consulting for women on an individual and full-time consulting basis. In the summer 2002, Chanin Richel became a reality.

Working from her home, Chanin started the company with solid strategic imperatives that propelled Chanin Richel into becoming a full-fledged fashion design firm. With a strong focus on quality designs and products, Chanin Richel quickly became the talk of the Richmond metropolitan area as a result of being featured in several regional publications.

In addition to our fashion products, Chanin and her mother developed a line of skin care products. The line of products features sugar and salt scrubs, body butter and many more items.

Additionally, a non-profit community outreach service called "BEAUTIFUL" for women and children in transitional housing due to domestic violence, recovering substance abuse and also loss of employment. These services provide an opportunity for those involved to gain valuable life "with style" skills. These life "with style" skills include, but are not limited to:

1. **Developing your Spirituality**
2. **Self-Respect**
3. **Wellness**
4. **Image**
5. **Finances**
6. **Interviewing Skills**
7. **Leadership Skills/Teamwork**
8. **Social Skills**
9. **Learning to Celebrate/Graduation**

We also partner with leading firms like Dress for Success.